WATER, COMMUNITY, AND THE CULTURE OF OWNING

Water, Community, and the Culture of Owning

Eric T. Freyfogle

The University of Utah Press

Salt Lake City

Publication of this keepsake edition is made possible in part by the Wallace Stegner
Center for Land, Resources and the Environment
S.J. Quinney College of Law
and by
The Special Collections Department
J. Willard Marriott Library

This lecture was originally delivered on March 22, 2017, at the 22nd annual symposium of
the Wallace Stegner Center for Land, Resources and the Environment.

 The Defiance House Man colophon is a registered trademark of The University
of Utah Press. It is based on a four-foot-tall Ancient Puebloan pictograph (late
PIII) near Glen Canyon, Utah.

LIBRARY OF CONGRESS CATALOGING-IN-PUBLICATION DATA
Names: Freyfogle, Eric T., author. | University of Utah. Wallace Stegner
  Center for Land, Resources, and the Environment. Annual Symposium (22nd :
  2017 : Salt Lake City, Utah)
Title: Water, community, and the culture of owning / Eric T. Freyfogle.
Description: Salt Lake City : The University of Utah Press, [2018] | Series:
  Wallace Stegner lecture series | "This lecture was originally delivered on
  March 22, 2017, at the 22nd annual symposium of the Wallace Stegner Center
  for Land, Resources and the Environment." | «Publication of this keepsake
  edition is made possible in part by the Wallace Stegner Center for Land,
  Resources and the Environment, S.J. Quinney College of Law, and by the
  Special Collections Department, J. Willard Marriott Library.»
Identifiers: LCCN 2017060276 | ISBN 9781607816324 (pbk.)
Subjects: LCSH: Water rights—West (U.S.) | Water-supply—Government
  policy—West (U.S.) | Right of property—West (U.S.)
Classification: LCC KF5569 .F74 2018 | DDC 333.33/9—dc23
LC record available at https://lccn.loc.gov/2017060276

Printed and bound in the United States of America.

FOREWORD

The Wallace Stegner Lecture serves as a public forum for addressing the critical environmental issues that confront society. Conceived in 2009 on the centennial of Wallace Stegner's birth, the lecture honors the Pulitzer prize-winning author, educator, and conservationist by bringing a prominent scholar, public official, advocate, or spokesperson to the University of Utah with the aim of informing and promoting public dialogue over the relationship between humankind and the natural world. The lecture is delivered in connection with the Wallace Stegner Center's annual symposium and published by the University of Utah Press to ensure broad distribution. Just as Wallace Stegner envisioned a more just and sustainable world, the lecture acknowledges Stegner's enduring conservation legacy by giving voice to "the geography of hope" that he evoked so eloquently throughout his distinguished career.

The 2016 Wallace Stegner Lecture was delivered by Professor Eric Freyfogle from the University of Illinois College of Law on the subject of "Water, Community, and the Culture of Owning." Focusing on our cultural tendencies to treat nature as a commodity and to disregard its inherent connections to human welfare, Professor Freyfogle argues for a new ethic that places value on maintaining healthy land and water systems. To do so, he prods us to begin thinking and acting as a community in terms of the common good, not solely on the basis of private interests and rights. Echoing Wallace Stegner, he reminds us that a society connected to the natural world is one that will endure for generations to come. His message is timely and provocative in these contentious times.

Robert B. Keiter, Director
WALLACE STEGNER CENTER FOR LAND,
RESOURCES AND THE ENVIRONMENT

WATER, COMMUNITY, AND THE CULTURE OF OWNING

We find ourselves these days in rather troubled times. Most evident, of course, is our fractured politics, which confronts us almost daily. Our political differences, though, no doubt sink roots in contemporary culture—as they always do—however difficult these roots might be to trace. In some way, our culture plays a mischievous role in our current malaise. One is tempted to presume that partisan clashes are linked to our cultural *differences*, and, of course, to an extent they are. My sense, though, is that our deeper troubles might actually have more to do with cultural elements that we share, with cultural traits, widely embraced by nearly all of us, that are ill-suited for where we find ourselves along our national trajectory. If I'm right, or even partly right, then we can't simply seek out some compromise position, some middle ground, politically or culturally. Indeed, our current disinclination to move toward a middle ground these days—our hyperpartisanship, we call it— might well reflect a sense that the middle ground isn't really appealing for anyone. No one likes what seems to lie in the middle. If this is so, this reality ought to be a revelation for us, a wake-up call. And what it might be telling us is that our problems permeate the whole political spectrum as we now conceive it and that a sensible path forward would lead us, not toward some middle place but to some really quite different one.

Our problems today, I want to suggest, show up when we talk seriously about water, about community, and about private property—the key words in my title. I want to comment on these three topics, weaving in and around them a bit and treating them not so much as three distinct topics but as variations on one topic. I'll conclude with some words about today's political morass and about the continuing relevance of Wallace Stegner.

We are having real trouble today interacting with fresh water. We don't have enough of it to satisfy all our desires. Decades ago, we would have talked about water *shortages* and how to increase supplies. These days, many of us are prone to think instead that the problem lies more on the other side, with excesses of demand.

Our water conundrum overall has two main components. One of them is environmental: we aren't leaving enough water in rivers and lakes to keep them healthy in ecological terms—not enough water overall, not water at the right times, and not water of good quality. We struggle with this environmental challenge for familiar reasons. As a people we tend to resist limits on our appetites and activities, whether self-imposed or pressed upon us by nature. Similarly, we don't worry about problems that aren't visible and immediate. And then, we're confident we know enough—that we have enough science, technology, and general smarts—to get us out of any messes. So we charge ahead.

The second side, or component, of our conundrum is that we've not been able to move water to higher-valued uses. We typically use the free market to move natural resources around; that's its principal job. But the market isn't really working when it comes to water flows, not well enough. We view water, or water rights, as commodities, and we expect commodities to move by market forces to users that pay the most money. But it isn't happening, and so we end up with extremely costly plans to desalinate seawater to meet urban needs while continuing to use massive water flows for hayfields or to grow grains already in oversupply. In my home state of Illinois we have far too much corn. We get rid of the surplus by turning it into ethanol in an overall process that consumes almost as much energy as it produces. As a matter of *national* priorities, we don't need to grow more corn using scarce water or more cotton or rice or hay crops.

What underlies and joins these two water problems, I believe, is their common origin in modern culture. They come about because strands or traits of our culture simply don't fit together with nature. When it comes to making sensible use of fresh water, the culture we have—the culture we've inherited, carried forward, and refined—isn't getting us to where we need to be—to healthy lands and rivers and to flourishing communities.

Our environmental ills are caused by the ways we interact with nature. Simply put, human behavior is always the cause. We know this, of course; we know that environmental problems aren't simply a matter of nature being nature. We humans are misusing it. So why do we misuse nature? Why do we behave toward nature as we do?

Our uses of nature, for good and ill, have something to do with our growing population, of course. They have much to do with our technology, particularly our harnessing of fossil fuels. But also at work—and perhaps even more important—is our culture. Our current population could live in harmony with nature if we chose to live differently. As for technology, it reflects who we are and what we want, and we can use it for good and ill. The key piece—according to environmental historians such as Donald Worster and J. R. McNeill—is within and among us, in our perceptual, intellectual, and moral orders. Our uses of nature are mediated by the ways we see nature and evaluate it and by the ways we understand ourselves in relation to it and to one another. If these historians are right—and I believe they are—we aren't going to find ways to use water sensibly by placing all our bets on science, technology, or market forces.

So what aspects of our culture seem problematic?

For starters, there's our tendency to fragment nature into pieces and to treat its pieces simply as commodities. As commodities, these natural fragments are mostly valued by the market, priced at what some person with money is willing to pay for them. By this metric, most parts of nature—including most species—are valueless and easily ignored.

Our thinking is quite short term: a few years, a few decades at most; future costs and benefits are discounted to the present; the long term—indeed, anything over fifty or seventy-five years—becomes almost irrelevant.

We profess to believe in Darwin and evolution but nonetheless continue to believe we are a life form that differs in kind from all other species. We humans are morally worthy, no other species is; we are moral subjects—actors—while the rest of nature is raw material for our manipulation. Human exceptionalism, it is termed.

As for ourselves, we are best understood—so we think—as autonomous individuals, as discrete living creatures, defined chiefly by our autonomy and moral agency, not by the ways we are interconnected and interdependent. This is the heart of liberalism, classically understood.

In our dominant liberal culture, our main moral principles—the normative frames we use to interpret our social life—are liberty, equality, and a few related individual rights. When debating public issues, we turn instinctively to this language of individual rights, which are held, of course, only by present-day living humans. These are narrow normative frames—liberty and equality—and they don't give much guidance for our dealings with nature. Liberty and equality have to do with the ways people relate to one another and to government, not to the ways people relate to land.

How then should we be living in and with nature? Clearly we can't survive without using nature, so it isn't sensible to halt all uses, to stop changing it. We can use nature, yes, but we shouldn't be abusing it, that's the idea.

So how do we distinguish between the two; how do we draw the line between the legitimate use of nature and the abuse of it? That's a foundational, normative challenge for us as earthly beings, and we aren't thinking clearly and broadly about it. We struggle with this intellectual and moral task in significant part because the normative language we share in public doesn't provide apt tools to do this work, to think and speak clearly about our rightful place *in nature*. We can argue all day about liberty and equality—we can throw in the language of safe streets and economic growth—and still not have the moral and prudential vocabulary appropriate for discussing good land use. We need a richer normative vocabulary, by which I mean a vocabulary having to do with good and bad, wise and foolish, moral and immoral—a vocabulary that expresses shared values and goals.

At present, our normative talk pretty much comes down to personal choices made by individuals. Think about standard economic analysis. At the base of it are the preferences of individuals. Give people what they want—that's the way economists talk about public policy—and more is always better. Think too about moral philosophy, where we find the same story. Utilitarian or consequentialist moral theories rest on maximizing preference satisfaction. Rights-based or deontological thinking is all about honoring individual rights, honoring personal choices, and operating under legal principles that apply equally to all. This is fine as far as it goes, but it doesn't help decide what we ought to prefer, individually and, even more, collectively. What forms of habitation, of dwelling in nature, should we value highest?

So what's missing here? What is our culture discounting or ignoring?

We can start with the many species of life—nearly all of them—that lack market value. Our economic thinking largely ignores them, except for the few individuals who do care and are willing to spend money to protect them.

Ecological interconnections and interdependencies are similarly discounted. As we fragment nature and sell off its parts, we fracture and disrupt ecological processes and connections. We degrade what we have come to call nature's ecosystem services. We disrupt the healthy functioning of the land as an ecological whole.

Future generations similarly are ignored, except, again, as individuals living today choose to take account of their interests.

Then there are the limits on our senses, our ways of learning about nature, and our overall understanding. There is much we do not know about nature, and our deficiencies go beyond simple uncertainty to outright ignorance. In our decision-making processes, we don't have good ways to take this ignorance into account, even when we confess it. Indeed, so strong is our commitment to liberty and to a free market we are prone to insist that those who do worry about problems—*they* need to prove their existence and with an astonishingly high level of confidence. We assume a problem does not exist—think climate change here—unless those who purport to see the problem can demonstrate it with scientific certainty. Scientific certainty! We're not talking here about preponderance of the evidence, not about clear and convincing facts, indeed not even about proof beyond a reasonable doubt. Scientific proof is higher still. We execute people with lesser levels of confidence. It is a misguided burden of proof—profoundly so. Yet we use it instinctively, giving evidence as we do so of just how high we exalt individual liberty and at what cost.

Let me turn to private property for a few minutes, especially private rights in nature. Property, as we know, is a legal institution. Ownership rights are prescribed by law. But property is also a central component of our culture, a formative institution that helps define who we are as a people. The United States is the land of private property; it is a key embodiment of our liberty. With property in hand, individuals can exercise their liberty and seek to satisfy their preferences; they can retreat to their private lands to enjoy their autonomy.

When we study private property as a constellation of cultural values what we find is that it comprises and accentuates the very cultural elements, just mentioned, that are root causes of our misuses of nature. Private property has distinct boundaries, which is to say it's based on the fragmentation of nature. Property can be bought and sold; it is nature turned into commodity. The value of property is set mostly by the market, which in turn reflects the preferences of people with money to spend—living people, not future generations, not other life forms. This fragmentation overlooks ecological processes and interconnections. As for good land use—what it means to live well on a tract of land—it is up to the owner to decide, based on personal preference. Use land as you like, just don't unduly harm your neighbors—that's the main message we give landowners, in rural areas particularly. Don't harm your neighbor because that would interfere with rights held by your neighbor. But otherwise, there is no overarching, normative standard to use in judging the choices a landowner makes. And we have no normative standard for the reasons just identified because our shared normative language is all about individual rights—liberty and equality above all—with a heavy dose of economic growth tossed in.

We fragment nature and treat it as commodities.

We discount or ignore interconnections, interdependencies, ecological functions.

Value chiefly means market value—value to living people with money to spend.

Other life forms and future generations count for little.

Owners can charge ahead as they like, exercising restraint only if and when they care to do so.

And mostly, to reiterate, the dominant moral language of our day concerns itself with rights-bearing individuals, understood as autonomous beings, legitimately out to satisfy their preferences in a market-centered world that rewards aggression and risk-taking.

This is the culture we have—the culture, I think, that we have ridden to where we are; to the good places, yes, and to bad places: to growing water shortages, to precipitous declines in world wildlife populations, to ecosystems degraded by excessive nitrogen, to expanding dead zones in estuaries, to barely controllable forest fires, and to a changing climate that promises massive ecological disruption.

What I hope you can see in this cultural snapshot is that these cultural elements do not reside at just one place on our national political spectrum. From one end to the other, we find people who embrace human exceptionalism and who comprehend humans as autonomous individuals. Rights—albeit somewhat different rights— are held high everywhere. Individual preferences are also honored everywhere, restricted only by clashes with the preferences of other individuals. Yes, there are those who lament environmental decline. Yes, there are those who attack economic inequality. But they have few moral principles or standards to wield in their fighting other than the principles or standards everyone else also has and also puts to use.

So what might a better culture look like, and what might all this mean for our water problems and the future of private property?

Surely we ought to have, as a shared normative goal, finding ways to live on land that keep the land, and us, healthy. This should be element one of the common good, transcending personal preferences. We ought to keep our actions on the good-use side of that vital line dividing legitimate land use from abuse. And we ought to be thoughtful and wide-ranging as we go about drawing that essential line, paying attention to the full range of relevant normative factors. The conservationist Aldo Leopold once termed this the "oldest task in human history"—the task of living on land without degrading it. We were not doing well at that task, Leopold lamented in the late 1930s. We struggle with it still.

A land-respecting culture would begin with the recognition that, like all life forms, we humans are embedded in natural systems. We are components of larger natural wholes—"plain members and citizens" of the land community, as Aldo Leopold put it. The land is an interconnected community of life, including its plants, animals, waters, rocks, soils, and people. That community can be more or less healthy in its functioning. The health of the whole—the health of the land community as such—should thus be a paramount value that we all share a polestar that guides how we live.

This means perceiving nature as a functional system and valuing it as an organic whole, not as a warehouse of raw materials. When we evaluate our landscapes and how well we are dwelling on them, we need to put the land's functional health first and stop thinking about it, as we long have, in terms of natural-resources flows or, even worse, cash-income flows to an owner. In nature's functioning, countless living creatures play key roles and have value as community members. Given this, and given our limited knowledge of land functioning, it's plainly prudent to keep around as many native and locally adapted species as possible.

When we add people to this picture of nature we need to see them—we need to see ourselves—also as members of this complex, interconnected biotic community. We too are embedded in nature, more than we commonly realize. We too are dependent for our long-term flourishing on the healthy functioning of natural systems. The land community of which we are a part can be more or less healthy. And we need it to be healthy; we need to live in ways that keep it healthy.

What if, day by day, our newspapers and news feeds gave us updated reports on the health of our natural communities, just as we get reports on the health of our economy?

The cultural shifts I've been describing are plenty challenging—overwhelming, some might say—new ways to see nature and to understand our place in it, a much stronger emphasis on the health of natural communities as such. But there is yet more of our culture that calls for repair. Also needing reform are some of the key ways we relate to one another. As I've just said, I believe we are wise at this point in our history to hold high, as a shared good, the ecological health of the land community. We need to see it as a good that transcends individual preferences. If we are all members of a larger community, whether we know it or not, then we are not just autonomous individuals bouncing about. We are fellow community members; we are interwoven, one to another, socially as well as to nature. The links among us—the social orders that we compose—are thus morally vital; they have value even though they cannot be bought and sold, value, again, that transcends the preferences of individuals acting alone. Communities, of course, last much longer than an individual life. And so when holding high our communities, we are naturally drawn to a longer-term perspective, one that gives membership and moral status to future generations.

When we see ourselves as comembers of larger communities, when we realize our long-term welfare depends on the good functioning of these communities, then land use and water use inevitably become matters of public business as well as private business. Land-use patterns are not good unless they sustain the healthy functioning of land systems in all their biological richness. Water-use patterns are similarly not good unless they uphold the healthy functioning of aquatic systems.

So what does this mean in terms of private property? As I've suggested, private property, in its important, cultural form, is an embodiment of key elements of our culture (or any culture)—the good elements and the bad. As a legal institution, property is highly flexible; it can take a wide variety of forms in terms of what can be owned and the rights and responsibilities that attach to owners. There is no single ideal or exemplary form of ownership. How we define property at law, then, is closely tied to the surrounding culture and its associated economy.

If we did make changes to our dominant culture—moving in a direction that valued communities as such, particularly the land community—we would no doubt see the need to update our much-loved institution of ownership. For starters, it is important to appreciate that private property can survive and work well even while we make fairly substantial changes in the ways the institution works. There is no single simple spectrum on which we can chart how well or how poorly various interest groups respect private property, with high respect and protection on one end and little respect and protection on the other. That's simply not right. Pretty much everyone in the United States supports private property. What's at stake—what we would be disagreeing about if we thought things through more clearly—are the elements of private ownership: what can be owned, how we might best define private rights, and, perhaps above all, how we might best tailor the rights of one owner to fit sensibly with the rights of other owners and with the rights of communities as such. It is entirely legitimate for us today to alter these elements of private ownership, just as generations in the past did when they were in charge of the institution.

The meaning of private ownership has shifted substantially over the past two centuries. When we look further afield, to other nations and further back in time, we encounter a rich array of private ownership arrangements, crafted by lawmakers to meet the needs and reflect the values and hopes of varied communities. Property is highly flexible. Like generations past, we can alter its elements so that it better supports our circumstances and hopes—and do so, moreover, without undercutting its core functions. Private property should be our collective servant, not our master.

A great deficiency of the contemporary environmental or conservation movement has been its failure to take property seriously, its failure to take time to understand this complex, flexible institution and see how we might reform it. Clashes over the meaning of private ownership are, at root, clashes over just the issues I've been talking about: how we see nature and our place in it, how we understand ourselves variously as autonomous individuals or as community members, whether we value community health as a shared good, and more.

For too long, the private property issue has been dominated by the self-styled property-rights movement. The movement offers up a vision of private ownership rooted in the values that have been dragging us down—a vision of ownership based not just on human exceptionalism and individual autonomy but on understandings of individual rights that detach them completely from any sound vision of the common good. This libertarian vision of private property is only one form property rights might take. Better ones are readily found.

There is no reason why the conservation movement should not stand solidly in favor of private property, and say so. What it ought to promote is an alternative vision of private ownership—one that reflects broader senses of value and that recognizes the ways one owner's actions affect others, near and far. The conservation movement needs to put forth a vision of *responsible* ownership, one that expects owners to use what they own in ways consistent with the health of natural and social communities, one that presents owners as community members and expects them to act accordingly. It can be done; it needs to be done. But it will happen only if the conservation movement takes property seriously, as an institution, a problem, and an opportunity.

For generations—for centuries—it was understood that private property is a morally complex institution. Think about its contradictory links to liberty. Private property, we hear, is a core protection for liberty; the more we protect property, the more we protect liberty, so it is said. But this is highly misleading, a stance that shows concern only for the welfare of the property owner. Yes, property can expand the liberty of an owner. But think of the wandering hunter who enters private land looking for food and is arrested and imprisoned for trespass; arrested, we need to note, by agents of government. For the hunter, this is a massive interference with individual liberty, and it's an interference by state actors. How can this be morally tolerable? We might say our hunter has been lawfully arrested for violating private property rights. But it is the very legitimacy of those property rights that is in question. What gives one person, wearing the label of property owner, the right to call on agents of the state to restrict the liberty of a fellow citizen?

It is possible to defend this use of state power, but only in a highly qualified way. I pose this conundrum not to answer it today, but simply to emphasize that private property is morally troubling, as philosophers have long known. The recurring philosophic question, generation after generation, was how to make the institution of ownership legitimate given that it comes at such high moral costs. Our cultural tendency is to assert glibly that private ownership is somehow an individual right that transcends the law. But this stance doesn't hold up—not morally, when you consider the conflicting rights of nonowners, and not jurisprudentially. Property is a product of law. Rights exist only to the extent recognized by law, laws that a lawmaking community has every right to alter. We can wield that power today to revise our ownership norms to keep the institution up to date, to keep private property from becoming what it often has been—and still is in much of the world—a tool of oppression and exploitation.

Private property is not some sort of private power. It is public power—police, courts, prisons—put at the beck and call of individual owners who use that power, or can use it if we let them, to dominate other people and frustrate the common good. We need to take property seriously. We need to take responsibility for it, in terms of its elements. When the rules governing property use get out of date, when it allows owners to act in ways that undercut the common good, then it becomes morally illegitimate.

Many of us have trouble with the notion that lawmakers can change the content of ownership rights, particularly in fundamental ways. How can that be, if property is an individual right? How can it be, given how our nation's founders put such stock in individual rights? What we forget, asking these questions, is that individual rights, since their emergence in the eighteenth century, were commonly understood as derivative of the common good. Rights existed to the extent they supported the common good; in fact, they were social tools for promoting that common good. And they still are, when sensibly defined and limited. The early liberal writer John Stuart Mill said this clearly: rights should be pruned when their exercise clashes with the public welfare. Oliver Wendell Holmes said the same thing with equal clarity. Yes, private property is a right, but it is a right that arises under a set of property laws crafted and kept up to date for the purpose of fostering the common good.

Let me turn back to water, about which I've had little to say directly but much to say indirectly. Generations ago, lawmakers realized that water was like wandering wildlife: it didn't stay put in one place and was therefore hard to divide up the way surveyors divided land. Out of this trait of nature came legal rules proclaiming that water and wildlife are owned by the people collectively. Water, like wildlife, is different. No one owns a water flow. What individuals can possess are limited rights to use water—rights that, like all property rights, should be crafted and updated to promote the common good.

It is in recognition of the public's paramount ownership of water that all private rights in water flows are expressly conditional. In some states water uses must qualify as reasonable. Elsewhere they must qualify as beneficial. So what do these terms mean? They're vague, to be sure. But what ought to be clear is that these terms—*reasonable* and *beneficial*—refer to the good of the community as such and based on today's circumstances and values. Reasonable means socially reasonable today, based on today's standards. Beneficial similarly means socially beneficial today, in light of where we find ourselves and how we assess our needs. *Reasonable* and *beneficial* do not refer to the benefits received by the owner. Nor can they sensibly refer to circumstances and values from decades or generations ago. A particular water use is beneficial only if it is a water use that the community today, if it were allocating the water, would recognize and support as socially beneficial. This is, I contend, the only definition of the term that is consistent with the public's paramount ownership rights, the only definition that keeps the private ownership of water rights morally legitimate. It also, importantly, aligns with the way the reasonableness test is applied in every other property law setting, including (to cite closely related examples) in public and private nuisance law, in drainage law, in reasonable-use versions of groundwater law, and in the law of riparian rights. In no setting does *reasonable* mean reasonable as of a century ago. Landowners everywhere must modify their practices to keep them reasonable to avoid claims of nuisance. Why should holders of prior-appropriation water rights escape this same socially and morally justified obligation?

Water law needs updating to reflect the new cultural values and understandings I've been discussing. We need to see water flows, better than we do, as indispensable parts of functioning ecosystems. With community health as our paramount goal, water flows must first meet the functional needs of aquatic and terrestrial ecosystems. We start with healthy rivers and lakes. Next comes water to meet the most vital of human needs for drinking water and immediate household use. This was the water law priority when our nation was founded under the old natural-flow version of riparian rights. It is recognized overtly in the most recent restatement of the law governing international watercourses, the Berlin Rules of 2004 put out by the International Law Association. All other water uses would come after that, to the extent water is available. Any remaining water needs to go to the uses that are the most socially important for us today.

Too many water uses are not reasonable and beneficial by this appropriate standard. This is particularly true of agricultural irrigation to produce crops that are in oversupply nationally. On this issue, we need to listen to our neoclassical economists. The public policy question is not whether corn, cotton, or alfalfa are important; of course they are. The question is about marginal production and marginal value. How much do we need that last bushel of corn or that last bale of cotton? Frankly, we don't need them at all, just as we don't need that last sheep grazing in wolf habitat. Of course we ought to find fair ways to curtail water uses that are no longer appropriate, no longer legally beneficial—fair to water users and to communities and taxpayers alike. But we can do that pretty easily once possessed of the will and culture to make it happen. (My proposal is appended to this lecture.)

We struggle to shift water to better uses because today's low-valued water uses are wrapped up in and protected by the culture of owning, by the mythology of private property. That is their only defense, and it is a defense, I have suggested today, that is flimsy. It ignores the public's paramount rights in water. It ignores how people today have the power to rewrite property norms to foster today's common good. It is not consistent with the most sensible understanding of beneficial use: a legal limit on water uses. Most of all, it is a defense rooted in contemporary cultural elements that are long overdue for reform. Water is a communal asset, communal property. How it is used is inherently public business.

We need to push away this mythology and see many of our water uses for what they are, wasteful and environmentally destructive. If we can strip away the mythology of private property, we can find ways to wind down these outdated water uses while showing consideration for the plight of the people engaged in them. There's no reason to expect the market to do this work for us. Indeed, our expectation of salvation by market forces is one of our cultural branches most in need of pruning.

Let me wind down by returning to my starting point: our distorted and confused political scene and the troublesome culture it reflects. We say we have two political approaches today—one conservative and one liberal. But that's not so, not if we take words seriously. More apt, as many point out, is that we have a liberal party and a neoliberal party. But that dichotomy sheds light only if we get clear on what we mean by *liberal*. What the term used to mean—and still means in Europe—is a political approach that accentuates the individual and frees the individual from as many constraints as possible. By that definition, we have two liberal parties. We might just term them *liberal party A* and *liberal party B*. Of course they differ, but not in their fundamental commitments to a worldview populated entirely by rights-bearing, autonomous humans out to get ahead individually and focused on the short term. No version of pure liberalism is sound today, particularly given our ecological ills—not party A, not party B, and not some AB blend.

Our commitment to liberal individualism began life in the mid-eighteenth century, erupted at the time of our revolution, and gained strength up to and through the Civil War. We've ridden this cultural train for a long time now, and much good has come from it, particularly from our civil rights campaigns. But we've traveled this route too far, and liberalism as an ideology never really worked when it came to land, water, and other life forms.

We need to chart a different course, one that honors the community as such, that recognizes and seeks to uphold the things we share and the communal ties and bonds that sustain the health of natural and social communities. We can't leave behind the hard-earned lessons of our civil rights efforts, but we also shouldn't view them, and the individualistic, rights-based rhetoric they employed, as adequate guidance for handling today's problems, environmental problems in particular. Our culture needs reform, and if and as we reform it, new political possibilities will open up.

When this College of Law decided to put Wallace Stegner's name on its now-renowned Center for Land, Resources and the Environment, I was pleased. Finally, I thought, somebody got it right.

I met Mr. Stegner only once, at an occasion that happened because the S.J. Quinney College of Law invited me, back in the summer of 1990, to come out and teach a class on federal lands. I thought it odd for the college to invite someone for that purpose from a state with essentially no federal lands, but I didn't quibble. While here, my wife and I got wind that a civic organization named the Coalition for Utah's Future was hosting a fund-raising event, up on the mountain, to honor Stegner. As avid admirers of his work, we jumped at the chance to attend and paid a good deal extra to meet him in person and get signed copies of his just released *Collected Stories*. It was a memorable event. Robert Redford showed up late, returning from a movie set in Cuba. And Stegner drew a lengthy, glowing introduction from a then relatively unknown writer, Terry Tempest Williams. Only when reading a Stegner biography years later did I learn that Stegner became quite ill that night and had to be rushed to the hospital. Even before then, as a young assistant professor of law at Illinois, I tried to enlist Stegner to write a contribution to a law review symposium I was helping to edit. I figured, why not go for the best? Stegner sent back a most gracious letter, hammered out on his mechanical typewriter, apologizing that he just couldn't do it. He was at work then on what became his novel *Crossing to Safety* and claimed that, at his age, he couldn't undertake two projects at once. Needless to say, I kept his letter.

I say that this law school got it right by honoring Stegner because Stegner was one who appreciated the importance of culture, just as he appreciated nature, and he knew we couldn't make sense of one without the other. He knew we had environmental problems because of the ways we interacted with nature and that we couldn't craft societies that would endure, particularly in semiarid lands—societies worthy of these great landscapes—without a culture that valued community and treated nature with respect.

The practice around the country when framing environmental programs is to dwell almost solely on matters of science and technology. Scientists run the places. People hardly enter the picture. Culture rarely comes up. On this foundational point Wallace Stegner got it right, and so did the University of Utah.

Afterword

Moving Water to Higher-Priority Uses

Set forth here in outline form is one legal strategy to wind down low-valued water uses, freeing up water flows for higher-valued ones. The strategy would be easy to administer (politics aside), would cut costs considerably, should encounter few constitutional challenges, and, reasonably handled, would bring vast environmental gains, all while stimulating privately arranged water transfers. The chief difficulty is cultural: it collides with the mythology of private property that surrounds and defends low-valued, environmentally degrading water uses.

First, under guidance put forth by the legislature, a state agency would identify the lowest-valued water uses, those that are least reasonable and beneficial. Although various factors might be used in this assessment, any formulation of "lowest valued" ought to respect economic realities. One easy method is to identify how much a water user would pay for an acre-foot of water each year to sustain the current use. Those who would pay the least should rank low.

Second, those engaged in the lowest-valued uses would be told that they must change their ways and be given a deadline to do so (perhaps five years). During that period, the user must either shift to a higher-valued water use or transfer the water to someone else who puts it to a higher-valued use.

Third, if the water user does neither by the deadline date, then the state would purchase the water right using its eminent domain power, freeing up the water for reallocation. Payment would be based on the value of that water in the (low-valued) use to which it has been put, calculated by estimating the amount the user could consistently pay for the water. Many current water users could not reasonably pay as much as $50 or $100 per acre-foot per year. Capitalized at around 4 percent, that would mean (assuming a water flow that is perpetually reliable) a one-time payment to the water user of twenty times what the water user could pay; that is, a one-time payment per acre-foot of $1,000 (for a user able to pay only $50) or $2,000 ($100). This ought to qualify as just compensation for constitutional purposes given that the rights holder has had adequate time to sell at a higher price.

Fourth, this process would continue, moving upward from the bottom to end the lowest-valued uses, so long as more water is needed to meet environmental goals and to satisfy new, higher-valued uses.

This strategy is more accommodating of the interests of water users than current law, properly understood, requires. Under current law—particularly in a reasonable-use state such as California—water uses automatically terminate when a water user fails to use water beneficially if not also reasonably. Those terms most sensibly mean beneficial and reasonable to society as such and in light of today's circumstances and values. By this definition—the only one consistent with the public's paramount ownership rights in water and with a morally legitimate property regime—today's lowest-valued water uses are not beneficial and reasonable. Under current law as thus understood, a court could (and, in a proper case, should) declare the rights void, giving the water user no time to make changes and requiring no payments to the owner.

In offering advance notice, opportunity to change, and fair compensation, this strategy is generous.

Further Readings

Given the wide-ranging nature of this talk, it was not possible to elaborate on the main points. The topics covered and the main stances presented are all ones I have explored in other writings over the years. Readers might turn to them for further considerations and citations to other authors.

I explore the institution of private property most fully in two books: *The Land We Share: Private Property and the Common Good* (Island Press, 2003) and *On Private Property: Finding Common Ground on the Ownership of Land* (Beacon Press, 2007). In terms of overviews, I survey the various elements of private rights in nature in the first chapter of *The Land We Share* and present and critique common cultural ideas about private property (*half-truths*, I term them) in chapter 1 of *On Private Property*. The many changes in American property law over time are taken up in chapters 2 and 3 of *The Land We Share*; in chapter 2 of *On Private Property* (which traces the decline of the one-time right of Americans to roam the unenclosed countryside, regardless of land titles); in "Property Law in a Time of Transformation: The Record of the United States," *South African Law Journal*, 131, pp. 883–921 (2014); and in "Land Use and the Study of Early American History," *Yale Law Journal*, 94, pp. 717–42 (1985). The many contradictory links between property and liberty are taken up in "Property and Liberty," *Harvard Environmental Law Review*, 34, pp. 75–118 (2010). The moral complexity of property and how it might be justified are approached in different ways in chapter 4 of *The Land We Share* and chapter 4 of *On Private Property*; the latter chapter pays particular attention to the ways the public as a whole can benefit from a property rights system in which the rights and limits of ownership are thoughtfully defined and kept up to date. The topic is also addressed in "Private Land Made (Too) Simple," *Environmental Law Reporter (News & Analysis)*, 33, pp. 10155–69 (2003). My broadest inquiry into the many links (positive and negative) between private property and human well-being is "Private Ownership and Human Flourishing: An Exploratory Overview," *Stellenbosch Law Review*, 24, pp. 430–54 (2013). Many writings about property make use of a popular fable about how property arose in early times through individual initiative; I offer a much different fable, rooting property in tribal practices, in "Private Property: The Story Retold," *University of Illinois Law Review*, 2004, pp. 445–61 (reprinted with modest changes as an epilogue in *On Private Property*). The foundational elements of ownership are also taken up in "Goodbye to the Public-Private Divide," *Environmental Law*, 36, pp. 7–24 (2006), a piece that considers how the categories of public land and private land are better understood as a continuum of ownership arrangements that mix public and private.

As for larger issues of nature and culture, they have occupied my attention for over three decades. I consider the cultural roots of our misuses of nature most fully in *A Good That Transcends: How US Culture Undermines Environmental Reform* (University of Chicago Press, 2017). I set forth a more systematic inquiry into our place in nature, standing back as best I can from modern culture, in *Our Oldest Task: Making Sense of Our Place in Nature* (University of Chicago Press, 2017). Also relevant are most of the chapters of *Agrarianism and the Good Society: Land, Culture, Conflict, and Hope* (University Press of Kentucky, 2007). The challenge of distinguishing the good use of land from land abuse is addressed most fully in chapter 2 of *Our Oldest Task*. Chapter 4 of that work offers my fullest critique of the limits of liberty, equality, and other liberal ideals as normative tools for making sense of our place in nature. Chapter 3 considers why we struggle so much to determine what moral principles should bind us collectively and which ones instead are better left to individual choice.

I take the environmental movement to task for failing to engage private property as an issue in chapter 4 of *A Good That Transcends* ("Taking Property Seriously"). My more wide-ranging critique of the movement is *Why Conservation Is Failing and How It Can Regain Ground* (Yale University Press, 2006).

As for water rights, I set forth my views on reasonable and beneficial use much more fully in "Water Rights and the Common Wealth," *Environmental Law*, vol. 26, pp. 27–51 (1996). The flexibility of prior appropriation law I explore in "Context and Accommodation in Modern Property Law," *Stanford Law Review*, 41, pp. 1529–56

(1989). A more wide-ranging moral assessment of all water law, East and West, appears as "Water Justice," *University of Illinois Law Review*, 1986, pp. 481–519 (1986).

About the Author

 Eric Freyfogle is Swanlund Chair and Professor of Law Emeritus at the University of Illinois at Urbana-Champaign, where he has long taught courses on natural resources and property law, environmental law and policy, wildlife law, conservation thought, and economic inequality. His many books include *On Private Property* (Beacon Press), *Why Conservation is Failing and How It Can Regain Ground* (Yale University Press), and *The Land We Share* (Island Press), as well as the newly released *A Good That Transcends: Why US Culture Undermines Environmental Reform* and *Our Oldest Task: Making Sense of Our Place in Nature*, both with the University of Chicago Press. He has lectured widely in the United States and abroad and held visiting positions at the University of Auckland, the University of Cambridge, and the Stellenbosch (South Africa) Institute for Advanced Study. Long active in conservation efforts, he currently serves on the boards of directors of the National Wildlife Federation and the Illinois-based Prairie Rivers Network.